# THE NEW EARTH

## HOW TO GET THERE!

Written by Kathi DeCanio
Illustrated by Phillip Ortiz

LET THE CHILDREN PRESS

The New Earth: How to Get There
Copyright© 2022 Kathi DeCanio

ISBN: 978-0-9892016-7-4

letthechildrenpress@gmail.com
letthechildrenpress.wordpress.com

*To Jesus, who offers us life through*
*His death and resurrection.*

*Thank you to my son, Matthew Maresco,*
*for his theological input to the*
*direction of this book.*

# God Wants to Live with Us

When God created the earth, He had a plan. He would create man and woman in His very own image so that He could live with them. He would be their God, and they would be His people.

*"So God created human beings in His image. In the image of God He created them. He created them male and female." (Genesis 1:27, ICB)*

*"Now God's home is with men. He will live with them, and they will be his people. God himself will be with them and will be their God." (Revelation 21:3, ICB)*

When God created Adam and
Eve, He gave them a special
place to live—a beautiful garden
in the land of Eden. In the
beginning, He would walk with
them in the cool time of the day.
God enjoyed being with Adam
and Eve! He created us to be
with us, and He wants us to be
with Him and share all things
with Him.

In fact, God wants the very best
for you and for me, which is why
He wants to share Himself with
us. He is the very best for us,
better than anything else.

*We know that in everything God
works for the good of those who
love Him. They are the people God
called, because that was His plan.*
*(Romans 8:28, NET)*

Because God is life, to be separate from Him is death.
This is why He wants there to be no separation between us and Him.

*"I am the Way, the Truth, and the Life."* (*John 14:6, ESV*)

God wants what is best for us, He is wiser than we are, and He knows that He is perfectly righteous—He always does what is perfect and right.

So what would happen if one day Adam or Eve suddenly decided they wanted to be separate from God? Right, they would not stay alive.

At first, all went well, and every evening they took long walks and talked. He taught them how to plant seeds and grow them into food. He explained so much about nature—the animals, trees, and plants—to them. There was so much to eat, they never had to think about that one tree.

After a while, Eve grew curious about the tree, and Adam said to her, "Eve, **don't even touch it** or you'll die!"

That made her really curious. They couldn't even touch it?

So for some time Eve would walk over and look at the tree. What was on the fruit that even touching it would kill her? God didn't make anything else in the Garden that would do that. Why this one tree?

One day as she was looking at the tree, another of God's creations spoke to her,

*"Did God really say you must not eat the fruit from any of the trees in the garden?"*

*"Of course we may eat fruit from the trees in the garden," the woman replied. "It's only the fruit from the tree in the middle of the garden that we are not allowed to eat. God said, 'You must not eat it or even touch it; if you do, you will die.'" (Genesis 3:1-2, NLT)*

Adam, was there, but he didn't say anything.

*"You won't die!" the serpent replied to the woman. "God knows that your eyes will be opened as soon as you eat it, and you will be like God, knowing both good and evil."(Genesis 3:4-5, NLT)*

Being curious, Eve reached out and touched the fruit, and, to her surprise, she didn't die!

That fruit really did look delicious. So she picked one off the tree. And still she didn't die! Adam didn't say anything. He just watched. Eve took a bite. It really was delicious, and she hadn't died! "See, Adam, God didn't tell you the truth! All this time He has kept the best fruit for Himself." She held the fruit out to him, and he reached out for it. He held it in his hands, and he didn't die, so he took a bite.

As he did, he remembered what God had really said to him before God created Eve, "*You may eat the fruit from any tree in the garden. But you must not eat the fruit from the tree which gives the knowledge of good and evil. If you ever eat fruit from that tree, you will die!*" (Genesis 2:16-17, ICB)

# Because we desire to do what we want, we can't live with God

Suddenly Adam felt something he had never felt before. He looked down at himself and realized he was naked. They looked around and saw a vine with large leaves. They wrapped the leaves around themselves. They felt a little better, but what would they do when God came to visit them?

That evening, the Lord came just like He always did, so they hid among the trees from Him. When God asked Adam where he was, Adam realized he couldn't really hide from God, so he called out, "Here I am! I hid because I was naked and ashamed."

"How did you know to be ashamed? You must have eaten from the tree I warned you not to eat. Now that you have done that, you know the difference between what is good and what is evil because you have felt the taste of death."

"Well, it wasn't my fault," said Adam. He pointed to Eve. "It was her idea, and You are the One who gave her to me."

Eve didn't want to be blamed, so she pointed to the serpent and said, "It was his idea! He tricked me."

God explained that the death of which He had spoken was separation from Him. Adam and Eve would have to leave the Garden of Eden and could no longer eat the fruit of the tree that gives life because, if they did, they would live with their shame continually. And, they would not walk with the Lord in the evenings again because His face was already shining so brightly that they couldn't even look directly at Him. It was like looking right at the sun!

God made them one promise. One day from Eve's family there would be born a son who would crush the head of the serpent. That serpent would bite His heel, but His foot would come down to crush the serpent's head once and for all time.

Then the Lord showed them how to kill some sheep and burn some of the meat as an offering to Him to cover their sin, as it were, just as He made them clothes from the sheep's skin to cover their bodies.

*"The Lord God made garments from skin for Adam and his wife, and clothed them. And the Lord God said, "Now... he must not be allowed to stretch out his hand and take also from the tree of life and eat, and live forever." (Gen. 3:22, NET)*

So the Lord sent them from the orchard in Eden to cultivate the ground from which Adam had been taken. After sending them out, He placed angel guardians and a fiery sword on the eastern side of the orchard to guard the way to the tree of life. (Genesis 3:21-24)

What about God's plan to be with humans forever? How sad! But God's plan was not over. There was more to come.

You see, the Father, Son, and Holy Spirit planned that at just the right time, Jesus would actually be born as a human baby. One of Eve's descendants would be His human mother, but by the Holy Spirit, God Himself would be His Father.

# Abraham's Promise

Thousands of years later, God spoke to a man named Abram. He told Abram that if Abram would leave his land and trust God to lead him to a new land, then God would make him the father of a great nation. He would give that nation a land of their own. And, all the other nations of the earth would be blessed through Abram's family.

Abram believed God would do that, so he and his wife left and traveled until the Lord said, "Here! Stop here! This is the place!"

*Then the Lord said to Abram, "Leave your country, your relatives and your father's family. Go to the land I will show you. I will make you a great nation, and I will bless you. I will make you famous, and you will be a blessing to others. I will bless those who bless you. I will place a curse on those who harm you. And all the people on earth will be blessed through you. (Genesis 12:1-3, ICB)*

God made a special promise to Abram, and He even changed his name to Abraham. He promised Abraham that his wife, Sarah, would have a baby boy, even though she was almost 90 years old!

Well, this son, Isaac, was born. When he grew up, he had two sons, Jacob and Esau. Then Jacob had twelve sons. Imagine that! Each son had a large family, but they all stayed together living in the same place, and they became a nation. People called them, "The sons of Jacob." Later they became known as the children of Israel because God changed Jacob's name to Israel.

Later, when God delivered the people of Israel from being slaves in Egypt, He made a special promise—covenant—with them. He gave them instructions how to live with Him instead of choosing death.

*"Today I have given you the choice between life and death...oh, that you would choose life so that you and your descendants might live. (Deuteronomy 30:19, NLT)*

He said, "I will place my Holy Tent among you. I will not turn away from you. I will walk with you and be your God. And you will be my people" *(Leviticus 26:11-12, ICB)*. Remember that? It was the Plan.

# David's Promise

The Lord's Plan kept unfolding. Hundreds of years later, the Lord made a special promise to a king of Israel named David. He was a great-great-many-times-great grandson of Abraham. This was another covenant! He promised that as long as David and his children and grandchildren continued to walk with Him, they would rule in Israel. And one day, one of David's many-times-great grandsons would rule not only Israel but the whole world forever!

Can you guess who that would be? Yes, Jesus! He would be part of the Plan! He would be the one God promised to Adam and Eve, a descendant of Eve who would crush the head of the serpent. He would be a descendant of Abraham through whom the Lord would bless all the nations. And, He would be a descendant of King David and would one day rule the entire world forever.

*You will ...give birth to a son, and you shall name Him Jesus. He will be great and will be called the Son of the Most High; and the Lord God will give Him the throne of His father David; and He will reign over the house of Jacob forever, and His kingdom will have no end."* (Luke 1:31-33, NASB)

# Israel's New Promise

When the people of Israel had continued to choose death rather than life, He promised that one day He would make a new covenant with them and He would write His laws on their hearts so that they would always choose life. He even promised a new earth where they would live together.

*"I will make new heavens and the new earth. And they will last forever," says the Lord. "In the same way, your names and your children will always be with me." (Isaiah 66:22, ICB)*

At just the right time, a child was born who would be the answer to each of these covenants—special promises— that God had made–with Adam and Eve, with Abraham, David, and the people of Israel.

# Jesus, the Promised One

When He was born, the angel of the Lord told his mother to name him Jesus, which means "God Saves," for He would save His people from their sins. He was human because His mother was Mary, but He was also the Son of God, because His Father was God.

Jesus did what Adam did not choose to do. He was able to do something that all the descendants of Adam and Eve could not do. Jesus chose life instead of death. He partnered with God in everything He did and said. He was the only One who didn't have to be separated from God forever.

*Jesus explained, "I tell you the truth, the Son can do nothing by himself. He does only what he sees the Father doing. Whatever the Father does, the Son also does. (John 5:19, NLT)*

When Jesus was about 30 years old, the Father sent Him to preach
about the Kingdom of God where God would live with His people.
For over three years, Jesus traveled throughout Israel, preaching about
the Kingdom and healing the sick, opening blind eyes and deaf ears,
making the lame walk again, even raising people from the dead.

*Now when the sun was setting, all those who had any who were sick with various diseases brought them to him, and he laid his hands on every one of them and healed them. (Luke 4:40, ESV)*

Then came the next stage of the Plan. Remember when God told Eve that the serpent would bite her Son's heel, but He would crush the serpent's head? That is what happened next.

Even though Jesus did so many miracles that proved His message was true, miracles that proved He was the One who had been promised by God to come, the spiritual leaders of Israel did not believe He was truly the One who had been promised.

They made their own plan, with the Roman soldiers, to crucify Jesus. But, they didn't know this was actually a part of the Plan of God! The high priest "...*advised the Jewish leaders that it would be good if one man died for the people.*" (*John 18:14, NIV*)

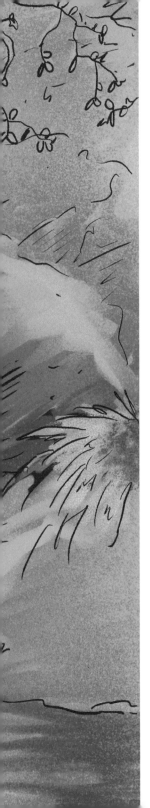

This was God's very plan! Jesus would experience death to take back the power of death over us so that we could once again have the opportunity to choose life and join the Lord in His kingdom on the New Earth forever.

And so Jesus, the Son of God/son of man, was put to death on a cross. His followers buried Him in a cave in the graveyard. And on the third day, He rose from the dead, just as He had promised He would.

The apostle Paul tells us, *"He was declared to be God's Son with great power by rising from death."* (Romans 1:4, ICB)

# How to Get to The New Earth

*So the great question is:*

How do we get to the New Earth where God's plan will be fulfilled and where He will live with us forever? How do we escape what God warned Adam about—the consequence of choosing death and separation from God?

In the same way that Jesus took up life again in His resurrection, He has invited us to take up life in Him. By the power of the Holy Spirit we can now join Jesus in doing only what He sees His Father doing.

This is easier than it sounds because the Holy Spirit has been sent to teach us and lead us in choosing life.

*I will put My Spirit within you and bring it about that you walk in My statutes.*
*(Ezekiel 36:27, NASB)*

We agree to the new covenant—God writing His laws on our heart—by believing that Jesus rose from the dead. Invite Him to write His laws on your heart and thank Him that He overcame death and invites you to overcome with Him, no longer choosing death, but choosing life and bearing the fruit of life.

*The fruit of the Spirit is love, joy, peace, patience, kindness, goodness, faithfulness, gentleness, and self-control; (Galatians 2:22-23)*

That's it! Then you live by doing what Jesus invites you to join Him in doing. After you die, Jesus will give you a resurrected body just like His so that you can live on the New Earth with Him forever.

NEW EARTH
THIS WAY

LET THE CHILDREN PRESS

CPSIA information can be obtained
at www.ICGtesting.com
Printed in the USA
BVHW021934200922
647535BV00001B/2